I0158963

FIRE Prayers
Prayers of Deliverance

EVANGELIST KING

Copyright © 2015 The Children's Mite. All rights reserved.

This book may not be copied or reprinted for commercial gain or profit. The use of short quotations, prayers or occasional page copying for personal or group bible study is permitted and encouraged.

Although every precaution has been taken to verify the accuracy of the information contained herein, the author and publisher assume no responsibility for any errors or omissions. No liability is assumed for damages that may result from the use of information contained within.

ISBN-13: 978-0692481271 (The Children's Mite)
ISBN-10: 0692481273

The Children's Mite

thechildrensmite.org

EVANGELISTIC OUTREACH

CONTENTS

ACKNOWLEDGEMENTS

I give ALL thanks to my Lord and Savior, Jesus Christ for His strength and loving mercy. Truly, if it was not for Him, I would have given up MANY times.

I thank God the Father through Him for His Spirit Who is my Helper, Comforter and Guidance.

AND

Those who are seeking the LORD God with ALL their heart, soul, strength and mind. Shalom †

PREFACE

What are FIRE Prayers?

FIRE prayers were revealed to Evangelist King by the Holy Spirit as she conducted deliverance sessions via the phone line or at the Holy Ghost FIRE Deliverance Meeting of *The Children's Mite*. According to James 5:16, they are proven to be effective and fervent in the spirit realm in setting captives free from spirit husband, spirit wife and EVERY spirit not of the Holy Spirit. If you have not done so already, follow us at www.vimeo.com/thechildrensmite and www.youtube.com/miteworks for more Holy Ghost FIRE Prayers (and videos). As the Holy Spirit leads and reveals, more prayer points will be added in Jesus' name.

What are Spirit Spouses?

Most people are unaware there are demonic spirit spouses-spirit husband and spirit wife. We know and understand about human spouses, but not spirit spouses. Our Heavenly Father created marriage for the human race which is honorable and the bed not defiled (Hebrews

1

13:4). Jesus says in his Word there is no marriage (Matthew 22:30) or gender (Galatians 3:28) in the spirit realm.

Satan does contrary to the will of God. Since God was the One who created and ordained marriage between a human male and female, Satan twisted this truth. He used for his glory the same concept, but for evil. He assigns spirit spouses to human beings in order to kill, steal and destroy their destinies in Christ Jesus. His aim is only to kill, steal and destroy (John 10:10).

Survey Questions

The survey is designed to reveal the existence of spirit husband and spirit wife, aka spirit spouses. Christ Jesus died for our FREEDOM (Galatians 5:1). He wants us to be totally free in our mind, free in our will, free in our emotions and free in our body to worship our Heavenly Father in spirit and truth (John 4:23-24). If you answer 'Yes' to any of the questions below, a spirit spouse is actively working in and against your life and hindering your destiny in Christ Jesus.

Do I Have a Spirit Spouse?

1.   Have you ever been molested? Molestation is not just restricted to penetration, but also include fondling by a child or an adult. It can be as simple as playing Mom and Dad games as a child or hearing someone talking in a sexual manner in childhood. I often stress to the person the

importance of asking the Holy Spirit to bring back to remembrance that which the LORD wants to be remembered because devils will block the person's memory in order to prevent exposure of the 'root' to their problem.

2. Have you ever been raped? A person can be raped by human beings, demon spirits and/or human spirits.

3. Do you have sexual lust?

4. Do you have sex in your dreams? Some people have sex in their dreams and are enjoying it. Dear Hearts that is not the Lord. If you have sex in your dreams and the person has the appearance of your spouse, it's not your spouse. It's a spirit spouse. It's not your human spouse. Or if it's a boyfriend or girlfriend, somebody you know. If you are even having sex in your dreams, period, dear heart, that is a demon spirit-a spirit spouse.

5. Does it seem like you're being "forced" to remain unmarried-every relationship ends up in disappointment? You've been engaged several times and each time for some reason, you have a change of mind. It's like you've been forced to stay unmarried. That's the sign of a spirit spouse.

6. Do you masturbate?

7. Do you watch pornography?

8.   Is there idolatry in your family lineage?

9.   Is there witchcraft in your family lineage?

These questions are evidences or signs of a spirit spouse; and only Jesus Christ with his chosen servant can set you totally free from that ungodly covenant of idolatry. Dear hearts, I've learned that it's good to allow the Holy Spirit to reveal the root cause of how spirit spouse entered into our mind, will, emotions and/or body. Knowing this truth, will help us to keep doors closed; and not only that, we are able to help others become free. Again, as you say the prayers out loud and experience any uneasiness or agitation, immediately contact us. You will need someone to join their faith with your faith for your complete deliverance in casting out the strong man (Mark 3:27). Praise the Living God!

FIRE PRAYERS

FIRE Prayers against Spirit Spouses (and friends)

Suppose a human thief or stranger was trying to break into your house? You wouldn't command them to leave your house quietly. You would shout out loud, "Get Out!" Likewise, the FIRE prayers need to be spoken out loud and aggressively. From your heart, say the FIRE prayers out loud:

1. Father, in the name of Jesus, YOU SAID when two or more are gathered in your Son's name, you are with us (Matthew 18:20).

2. Father, in the name of Jesus, YOU SAID whatsoever I bind or loose on earth; You will bind or loose in heaven (Matthew 18:18).

3. Right NOW, in the name of Jesus, SPIRIT SPOUSE, I COMMAND YOU to COME OUT of my mind, COME OUT of my will, COME OUT of my emotions and COME OUT of my body!

4. I bind, in the name of Jesus, EVERY spirit that is

not of the Holy Spirit and cast you at my Heavenly Father to deal with as He wills.

5. Spirit spouse, PACK YOUR LOAD AND GO, in Jesus' name!

6. By faith, I take the SCISSORS of God and cut and sever the spiritual umbilical cord of ungodly covenant and contract of witchcraft and idolatry!

7. I command spiritual poison to COME OUT of my stomach and body in Jesus' name!

8. Spirit snake, COME OUT!

9. Spirit Jezebel, COME OUT!

10. EVERY spirit not of the Holy Ghost, COME OUT!

11. By faith, I take the BLOOD OF JESUS and pour over EVERY known and unknown covenant and contract in the name of Jesus. Disconnect in Jesus' name!

12. Father, send your angels in the spirit realm and grab EVERY spirit that is not of You and send them where You desire to send them in Jesus' name.

13. HOLY GHOST FIRE, BURN! Burn everything that is not of You.

14. HOLY GHOST FIRE! HOLY GHOST FIRE! BURN! BURN! BURN!

FIRE PRAYERS

15. Holy Ghost give me a CLEAN SWEEP!

16. Give me a CLEAN FLUSH by Your MIGHTY FIRE in Jesus' name!

17. RANSACK OR SEARCH my mind!

18. RANSACK OR SEARCH my will!

19. RANSACK OR SEARCH my emotions!

20. RANSACK OR SEARCH my body! In Jesus' name.

21. Give me a CLEAN Flushing!

22. Give me a CLEAN Sweep!

23. Holy Spirit, leave no compartment or area untouched by your MIGHTY FIRE!

24. FIRE! FIRE! FIRE! BURN! BURN! BURN!

25. BURN from the crown of my head to the sole of my feet!

26. BURN! BURN! BURN!

27. FIRE Power of the Holy Ghost, set ABLAZE EVERYTHING not of you in Jesus' name!

28. Set ABLAZE! Set ABLAZE! Set ABLAZE!

29. FIRE! FIRE! FIRE!

30. THANK YOU, Father. My mind is NOW FREE to serve You. My will is NOW FREE to serve You! My emotions are NOW FREE to serve You. My body is NOW FREE to serve You. Father, fill me to overflow with your precious Spirit. Fill EVERY void and empty space in me by your mighty power of the Holy Ghost. Father, I thank you! I'm FREE!

Dear Hearts, if you experienced any uneasiness, agitation; and/or you just don't want to say the prayers, you need to submit the Deliverance Request Submission Form located on our website. There's a strong man in you that needs to come out and you need someone to join their faith with your faith. Someone who will believe God's Word for your total deliverance. Someone who God has appointed and anointed in coming against and throwing out the strong man. That's if you experience any uneasiness or agitation or if you didn't want to say the prayers. Again, there is a strong man in you that need to come out of God's house (the mind, will, emotions and body). Remember, the soul (mind, will and emotions) that sins is the one that will die (Ezekiel 18:20).

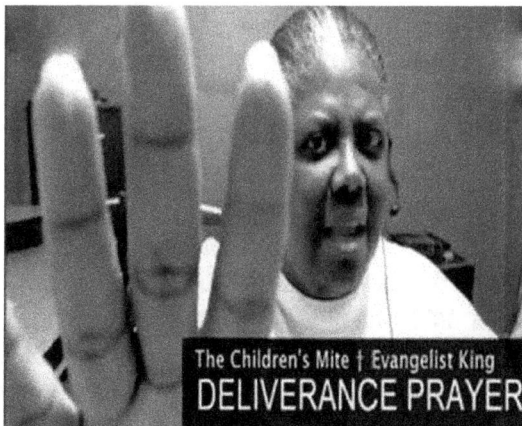

The Children's Mite † Evangelist King
DELIVERANCE PRAYER

Father, you said where two or three are gathered together in your Son's name, you are in the midst. You said whatever we bind and loose on earth, you will bind and loose in the heavens. Father, we also know there is no such thing as distance in the spirit realm. Father, I thank you right now for the one coming in agreement for their healing and deliverance in Jesus' name. Father, I thank you that right now through this book you are cleaning and rearranging your house in the mind, will, emotions and body and driving out EVERY spirit that doesn't move, walk, talk, act or sound like you. Father, in Jesus' name, I thank you for the mighty FIRE POWER of the Holy Ghost.

Right now, in the name of Jesus, I take my authority and command spirit lover, spirit husband, spirit wife and EVERY spirit not of the Holy Ghost to come to attention! You pack your load and get out! Get out of their mind! Get out of their will! Get out of their emotions! Get out of their body! In Jesus' name! Holy Ghost FIRE all over their body! Holy Ghost FIRE in their mind, in their will, in

9

their emotions! Holy Ghost FIRE burn everything that is not of you. Clean and sweep the house by your mighty FIRE! FIRE of the Holy Ghost! BURN in Jesus' name! Loose and leave God's property, you spirits of killing, stealing and destruction, in the name of Jesus!

The Blood of Jesus separates, detaches and disconnects everything that Satan has connected in their mind, in their will, in their emotions and in their body. Holy Ghost FIRE continue to consume everything that is not of you! Clean the house in Jesus' mighty name! Disconnect everything not of you! Separate and detach them from every known and unknown covenant of idolatry and witchcraft by the Blood of Jesus. Come out! Holy Ghost FIRE continue to burn and sweep the house clean. Leave no area or compartment untouched by your mighty FIRE. Holy Ghost FIRE continue to burn everything that's not of you out of the mind! Come out and pack your load and GO in Jesus' name! Never to return, physically or spiritually, in the name of Jesus!

Father, fill them to overflow with your Spirit. Let them feel your love, warmth and compassion in Jesus' name. Fill their mind. Fill their will. Fill their emotions. Fill their body. In Jesus' name. Father, I thank you for the angels you have dispatched right now to gather EVERY spirit that doesn't walk, talk or sound like you, and dealing with them and putting them where you desire. Father, I thank you for your fiery protection of the Holy Ghost. Father, thank you for filling them with your FIRE and protecting all their properties. Father, give them peace in their heart, mind, will, emotions and body in Jesus' mighty name. Thank you, Father, in Jesus' name. Amen.

WORDS OF ENCOURAGEMENT

IF you received the FIRE Prayers by and in faith, dear heart, you are now free. You are free from any internal interruptions and preventions that hindered your progress in life. You are free from devils living in your mind, will, emotions and body-forcing you to sin against God. You are free! Now, walk by faith and live by faith in the Son of God. Stay free! Submit your life to the Lord in all your ways. Be obedient unto his commands. Make sure you join a local church where the pastor is leading you back to your Lord and Savior, Jesus Christ. Walk in your new found freedom in Christ Jesus. Worship and magnify him! Thank him because he did not have to do it, but he did. Thank him for freeing you. Thank him for his mercy and grace. Thank him. He's there with you now. Praise his holy name. Say, thank you Jesus, thank you, and always receive of him by faith in Jesus' name.

Christ Jesus sets us free, but we MUST maintain our deliverance. Remember, the Deliverer said, "When an unclean spirit comes out of a person, it travels through dry country seeking rest and does not find it. Then it says to itself, 'I will return to the house I left.' When it arrives, it finds the house standing empty, swept clean and put in order. Then it goes and takes with it seven other spirits more evil than itself, and they come and live there-so that in the end, the person is worse off than he was before."

Dear Hearts, remembering these steps in James 4:7, SUBMIT-RESIST-FLEE, will help us to maintain our deliverance. Stay submitted in Jesus' name. Shalom.

TESTIMONIES

Good day. How are you and your family? I hope fine. I would like to share my testimony on how God delivered me from a spirit husband. Last night, I was listening to the podcast on, "Fire Prayers against spirit spouses and friends", and as you prayed these prayers, though I did not manifest, I felt the peace of the Lord flood my soul, and I received by faith that I had been delivered of these wicked spirits. I just want to firstly say, Thank you Heavenly Father for my deliverance, in Jesus' Name" and I also want to say thank you Evangelist King for letting God use you to set the captives free. I ask God to bless you and your household abundantly, in the Mighty Name of Jesus Christ, Amen.—Annette (USA)

I would like to say thank you thank you thank you. It is through your audio prayer for spirit spouses, and our heavenly father and Jesus that I have felt peace. While listening to it, I felt a tug at my heart and my mind was filled with the vision of shadows slipping away from me. I knew these were attached to me somehow. Afterwards, I felt stronger and more at peace with myself. I know something miraculous and wonderful happened when I listened to you that day, and is still happening. Thank you. Praise the Lord and may he continue his great work through you.—Mel (UK)

I went through the fire prayers for deliverance from a spirit spouse. I just wanted to have someone join their faith with me and any other deliverance necessary. Thank you all so much, in advance.—Nikki (USA)

Evangelist King, I heard about you from my daughter and I downloaded the Fire Prayers. My daughter prayed over me and I couldn't sleep last night so I'm requesting that you pray over me again to ensure deliverance from this "Spirit Husband". I want deliverance so that I can be a living witness to God and others that "whom the Son sets free is free indeed. Thank you for your attention to my request and may God bless you and your husband for the awesome work you all are doing for God's Kingdom.— Barbara (USA)

Kindly find attached the translation in Armenian of "Do I Have a Spirit Spouse?" prayer. I thank Lord Jesus from my heart for the deliverance he gave me by your prayers and I thank you also for your care and help. May Jesus bless you more and more, dear Terry. While translating it, I had to read it over and over and yawned all the time till tears flew down my eyes and I was filled with peace and joy.—Arshag (Lebanon)

I just said the prayers. I've had dark shapes follow me wherever I've lived. I don't know if I feel agitated after saying the prayer, but my nerves are trembling a bit.— Anne (USA)

FIRE PRAYERS

As I says these prayers, I began to burp and my fingers begin to feel numb, uneasy in my chest. I also notice that I had to force myself to listen and continue the prayers.—Althea (UK)

I have heard some deliverance prayers online during the last days and therefore believe that I need deliverance.—Monja (Armenia)

CONTACT US

Dear Hearts, I would love to hear your testimony. Go to our website and submit your testimony. I would love to hear your story, hear what God has done. Some of you, as the FIRE prayers were spoken, there were manifestations as demons were leaving. I want you to share that. Those of you who didn't and you felt the peace of God, you have to remember it is still God. God is the one who chooses whether he is going to allow demons to make themselves known or not. Many of you were set free and the demons left quietly. They came into you quietly, they left quietly and you felt the presence of the peace of God. I want to hear your testimony.

It encourages me when I read your testimony; because you need to realize that this work is by faith. I cannot see you and it's good to read testimonies. It's by faith that I know God's done what he said he would do. I want to hear your testimony. Remember, we overcome the devil, not only by the Blood of the Lamb, but also by the word of our testimony. We share our testimony, one with another, about the great things Jesus has done for us. We encourage each other in the Faith. It also encourage others in letting them see that the same God who set you free will set them free. So dear hearts, let us know your testimony and how helpful the prayers of deliverance were to you.

We are available to give one-on-one deliverance session from demonic bondages. MANY have come to us and the LORD God has set them totally FREE from spirit spouses and their friends. If you desire to be contacted, please be sure to fill out the required information on the form located on our website. Due to the volume of requests, we may not contact you as quickly as you desire; but rest assured, one of our Team Members will contact you.

REMEMBER, ALL DELIVERANCE SESSIONS ARE FREE, RECORDED AND CONFIDENTIAL (UNLESS YOU GIVE YOUR PERMISSION FOR US TO SHARE).

Again, thank you and praise His holy name. Shalom †

ABOUT THE AUTHOR

Mrs. Terry B. King aka Evangelist King continues to answer the supernatural call of and by God, to do the work of an evangelist through *The Children's Mite*, a ministry of salvation, healing, deliverance and giving, with outreach ministry that includes deliverance and feeding programs, as well as healing and deliverance services. She is Founder and CEO. Gifted with a compassion for the lost and neglected, she strives to share the "Good News" of Christ Jesus with everyone she meets. Understanding the Word of the LORD God through His anointed servants, "The work I'm doing in you, no man will be able to get the glory," she continues to strive to share the "Good News" of her Risen LORD Jesus to a physical and spiritual impoverished world.

Evangelist King has also authored, "The Children's Mite", "Holy Ghost FIRE Talk (Volume 1)", "Selah †" and several e-books. Check our website for more information.

www.ingramcontent.com/pod-product-compliance
Lightning Source LLC
Chambersburg PA
CBHW060605030426
42337CB00019B/3617